Campfire Cocktails

13-Digit ISBN: 978-1-64643-434-3
10-Digit ISBN: 1-64643-434-X

This book may be ordered by mail from the
publisher. Please include $5.99 for postage
and handling.

Please support your local bookseller first!

Books published by Cider Mill Press Book
Publishers are available at special discounts
for bulk purchases in the United States
by corporations, institutions, and other
organizations. For more information, please
contact the publisher.

Cider Mill Press Book Publishers
"Where good books are ready for press"
501 Nelson Place
Nashville, Tennessee 37214

cidermillpress.com

Typography: Livermore Script ATF,
Metallophile Sp8

Image Credits: Page 206 courtesy of Cider Mill
Press. Nature photography from Unsplash.com
and Pexels.com. All other photos used under
official license from Shutterstock.com.

Vectors used under official license from
Shutterstock.com.

Printed in Malaysia

23 24 25 26 27 COS 5 4 3 2

First Edition

CAMPFIRE COCKTAILS

100+ Simple Drinks for the Great Outdoors

CIDER MILL
PRESS

BOOK
PUBLISHERS

CONTENTS

INTRODUCTION

Camping has gained in popularity of late, and it has also splintered into numerous factions. There are those who spend days hiking into the extreme wilderness intending to live in their tent for weeks. There are those who seek out the most picturesque vistas, excited by the wonder and the images they'll be able to provide. There are those who, every weekend, load up the RV and head to the spot they've been renting for years. And there are glampers—those who want to get away without also having to do without.

But despite their massive differences in approach, the majority of these folks can agree on this: few things are better than sitting around a campfire with friends and/or family, a good cocktail, and great conversation.

A great time in the great outdoors really isn't much more complicated than that.

The key to making sure the cocktail component of that equation is on point is to remain similarly uncomplicated. While the modern mixology revolution has produced no shortage of memorable drinks, those involved syrups, cordials, and tinctures aren't what you're looking for when making drinks while camping. The reason for this is, whether you're carrying your supplies on your back or transporting them in a car, space is going to be limited.

Because of this, a good approach to making cocktails while camping is to batch them. Instead of just making one drink at a time as you would at home, simply maintain the ratios suggested in each recipe and multiply the amounts by the number of drinks you want. This method will allow you to bring fewer bottles, which means more room, either in the pack for food, or in the cooler for ice.

Due to the many different preferences and approaches, this book will be a lot more lenient in terms of glassware and garnishes. How the drink tastes and the company it is enjoyed in are far more important concerns than the vessel. If you're able to safely transport Nick & Nora glasses wherever you're going, by all means, tote them along. But one shouldn't hesitate to strain their concoction into a camp mug, mason jar, or whatever hardy container you rely on while camping. And while garnishes add an important aesthetic and aromatic element, they aren't so essential that one should bring them instead of actual food, ice, or a valuable piece of equipment.

Everything else is easy, so long as you remember that a campfire, a cocktail, and conversation is always a recipe for a memorable occasion.

WHISKEY

There is something about the woods that cries out for whiskey. Perhaps it is the warming and comforting character that whiskey always seems to carry. Perhaps it is its complex flavor, which goes well with the contemplative moments that arise from staring into a campfire. Whatever it is that you appreciate about whiskey, these cocktails will provide it, utilizing everything from smoky Scotch to spicy rye.

Old Fashioned

Traditionally, you'd use caster sugar in an Old Fashioned, but as Simple Syrup is easier to handle out in the wilds, a slight break from custom is called for.

1 teaspoon Simple Syrup (see opposite page)

2 to 3 dashes of bitters

Dash of water

2 oz. bourbon or rye whiskey

1 strip of lemon peel, for garnish

1 maraschino cherry, for garnish

1 Place the syrup, bitters, and water in a glass and stir until the sugar has dissolved.

2 Add ice and the whiskey to the glass and stir until chilled.

3 Garnish with a strip of lemon peel and a maraschino cherry (if desired) and enjoy.

Simple Syrup

Named due to its humble components—equal parts sugar and water—and the ease of making it— just place the sugar and water in a saucepan, stir as it comes to a boil in order to help the sugar dissolve, and then let it cool—there is nothing basic about the role simple syrup plays in cocktail making. Whether it is there to offset the lemon or lime juice, allow a tucked-away flavor to surface, or add body and viscosity to a drink, simple syrup definitively transcends its modest construction.

Boulevardier

The Negroni's surge in popularity makes most think that the Boulevardier is a riff, but it stands in a universe all its own. It's also quite good with a smoky Scotch in place of the bourbon.

1 oz. bourbon

1 oz. Campari

1 oz. sweet vermouth

1 orange twist, for garnish

1 Place the bourbon, Campari, and vermouth in a mixing glass, fill it two-thirds of the way with ice, and stir until chilled.

2 Strain over ice into a glass, garnish with an orange twist (if desired), and enjoy.

Rob Roy

While a campfire suggests that you employ the smoky Scotches Islay is famed for, don't shy away from experimenting with different Scotches—there's plenty of room to explore in this cocktail.

2 oz. Scotch whisky

1 oz. sweet vermouth

2 drops of Angostura Bitters

Luxardo maraschino cherries, for garnish

1 Place the Scotch, vermouth, and bitters in a mixing glass, fill it two-thirds of the way with ice, and stir until chilled.

2 Strain into a glass, garnish with maraschino cherries (if desired), and enjoy.

Walk the Night

The sweet spice of rye whiskey makes a complex match for the tart cranberry juice.

2 oz. rye whiskey

2 oz. cranberry juice

Splash of Simple Syrup (see page 11)

Dash of Angostura Bitters

1 maraschino cherry, for garnish

1 Place the rye, cranberry juice, syrup, and bitters in a cocktail shaker, fill it two-thirds of the way with ice, and shake vigorously until chilled.

2 Strain over ice into a glass, garnish with a maraschino cherry (if desired), and enjoy.

Irish Coffee

Being away from it all means you can spruce up your morning coffee without thinking twice.

3 oz. freshly brewed coffee

Dash of sugar

1 oz. Irish whiskey

1 oz. Irish cream liqueur

Whipped cream, for garnish

1 Pour the coffee into a glass, add the sugar, and stir until the sugar has dissolved.

2 Stir in the whiskey and liqueur, garnish with whipped cream (if desired), and enjoy.

Irish Coffee, see page 17

Brother Sparrow

Sweet, tart, and just enough spice to make each sip a memorable journey.

2 oz. rye whiskey

4 oz. lemonade

2 oz. cranberry juice, to top

1 Pour the rye and lemonade over ice into a glass and stir until chilled.

2 Top with the cranberry juice and enjoy.

Muleskinner Blues

One of Dolly's best tunes gets honored in this variation on the Moscow Mule.

2 oz. Tennessee whiskey

¼ oz. fresh lime juice

6 oz. ginger beer

1 lime wheel, for garnish

1 sprig of fresh mint, for garnish

1 Pour the whiskey, lime juice, and ginger beer over ice into a glass and stir until chilled.

2 Garnish with a lime wheel and a sprig of mint (if desired) and enjoy.

Pomegranate Smash

The tannins in pomegranate juice produce a tart character that cuts beautifully against the bourbon's sweetness.

2 oz. bourbon

1 oz. pomegranate juice

½ oz. fresh lime juice

½ oz. honey

Pomegranate seeds, for garnish

1 Place the bourbon, juices, and honey in a cocktail shaker, fill it two-thirds of the way with ice, and shake vigorously until chilled.

2 Strain over ice into a glass, garnish with pomegranate seeds (if desired), and enjoy.

Summer Came Early

A good one for those glorious days that arrive at the end of May.

1 oz. fresh lemon juice

1 teaspoon Simple Syrup (see page 11)

1½ oz. bourbon

Club soda, to top

1 lemon slice, for garnish

Fresh mint, for garnish

1 Place the lemon juice and syrup in a glass and stir to combine. Add ice and the bourbon and top with club soda.

2 Stir the cocktail gently, garnish with a slice of lemon and mint (if desired), and enjoy.

Blackberry Pie

Berries and fresh herbs have a remarkable affinity for one another, a reality this cocktail takes full advantage of.

2 blackberries, plus 1 for garnish

1 sprig of fresh sage, plus 1 for garnish

½ oz. Demerara Syrup (see below)

2 oz. bourbon

1 Place the blackberries and sage in a cocktail shaker and muddle the mixture.

2 Add the syrup, bourbon, and ice and shake until chilled.

3 Strain over ice into a glass, garnish with an additional blackberry and another sprig of fresh sage (if desired), and enjoy.

Demerara Syrup

Place 1 cup water in a saucepan and bring it to a boil. Add ½ cup demerara sugar and 1½ cups sugar and stir until they have dissolved. Remove the pan from heat and let the syrup cool completely before using or storing.

Hissing of Summer Lawns

As fresh and calming as listening to the evening wind in the trees following a day of hiking.

1 oz. fresh lemon juice

6 fresh basil leaves, plus more for garnish

1 oz. Simple Syrup (see page 11)

2 oz. rye whiskey

1 Place the lemon juice, basil, and syrup in a glass and muddle.

2 Add the rye and ice, stir until chilled, garnish with additional basil (if desired), and enjoy.

Play the Ghost

The honey takes care of the Tabasco's spice, allowing its deep flavor to come through in full.

1½ oz. bourbon

¾ oz. Honey Syrup (see opposite page)

½ oz. fresh lemon juice

Dash of Tabasco

1 strip of lemon peel, for garnish

1 Place the bourbon, syrup, lemon juice, and Tabasco in a cocktail shaker, fill it two-thirds of the way with ice, and shake vigorously until chilled.

2 Strain over ice into a glass, garnish with a strip of lemon peel (if desired), and enjoy.

Honey Syrup

Place 1 cup water in a saucepan and bring it to a boil. Add 1 cup honey and cook until it is just runny. Remove the pan from heat and let the syrup cool before using or storing in the refrigerator.

Looking Glass

This cooled-down toddy will serve you well on those evenings when it remains hot even after the sun's gone down.

1 oz. bourbon

1 oz. lemonade

1 oz. Honey Syrup (see page 33)

¼ oz. fresh lemon juice

1 lemon slice, for garnish

Fresh mint, for garnish

1 Place the bourbon, lemonade, syrup, and lemon juice in a cocktail shaker, fill it two-thirds of the way with ice, and shake vigorously until chilled.

2 Strain over ice into a glass, garnish with a slice of lemon and fresh mint (if desired), and enjoy.

Le Bon Temps

A no-fuss cocktail that encourages those rare moments when everything falls into place.

½ lemon, cut into wedges

4 fresh mint leaves

2 oz. bourbon

⅔ oz. ginger beer

1 Squeeze the juice of the lemon wedges into a glass and then drop the squeezed wedges into the glass.

2 Add the mint, muddle, and add ice.

3 Add the bourbon, top with the ginger beer, stir until chilled, and enjoy.

Whiskey Sunset

A white wine that resides toward the drier end of the sweetness spectrum will serve you well here.

2 oz. bourbon

2 oz. white wine

1 oz. lemonade

Splash of Simple Syrup (see page 11)

3 oz. ginger ale

1 lemon wheel, for garnish

1 Place the bourbon, wine, lemonade, and syrup in a glass, add ice, and stir until chilled.

2 Top with the ginger ale, garnish with a lemon wheel (if desired), and enjoy.

Ice Age

For those muggy mornings when a cup of spiked hot coffee just won't do.

Splash of Simple Syrup (see page 11)

Dash of Peychaud's Bitters

2 oz. bourbon

4 oz. iced coffee

1 Place all of the ingredients in a glass, add ice, stir until chilled, and enjoy.

Teatime Down South

Those who like their cocktails sweet get all they could ever dream of in this iced tea–based serve.

½ oz. fresh lemon juice

2 fresh mint leaves

1½ oz. bourbon

6 oz. sweet iced tea

1 lemon wheel, for garnish

1 Place the lemon juice and mint in a glass and muddle.

2 Add the bourbon, sweet tea, and ice and stir until chilled.

3 Garnish with a lemon wheel (if desired) and enjoy.

Hot Toddy

A drink capable of matching the comfort provided by the campfire.

2 oz. blended
Scotch whisky

½ oz. fresh
lemon juice

¼ oz. Simple Syrup
(see page 11)

Boiling water, to top

1 lemon slice,
for garnish

1 cinnamon stick,
for garnish

1 Place the Scotch, lemon juice, syrup, and water in a
mug and stir to combine.

2 Garnish with a lemon slice and a cinnamon stick
(if desired) and enjoy.

Old Reliable

A good one for when you're getting back together with the college crew, as the orange liqueur adds depth to a drink that was no doubt a standby: the Whiskey & Coke.

2 oz. whiskey

6 oz. cola

1 oz. orange liqueur

Splash of fresh lime juice

1 orange wheel, for garnish

1 Place the whiskey, cola, orange liqueur, and lime juice in a glass, add ice, and stir until chilled.

2 Garnish with an orange wheel (if desired) and enjoy.

Wake-Up Cider

A bubbly cocktail that will clear away the cobwebs and get you excited about what's to come today.

1 oz. rye whiskey

2 oz. apple cider

1 oz. sparkling cider

1 Pour the rye and apple cider over ice into a glass and stir until chilled.

2 Top with the sparkling cider and enjoy.

A Frequent Flame

The bitters hold this sweet, smoky, and complex drink together.

Dash of Angostura
Bitters

½ oz. maple syrup

1 oz. Islay Scotch
whisky

1 oz. bourbon

1 orange twist,
for garnish

1 Place the bitters, syrup, Scotch, and bourbon in a mixing glass, fill it two-thirds of the way with ice, and stir until chilled.

2 Strain into a glass, garnish with an orange twist (if desired), and enjoy.

Jack & Ginger

In the outdoors, sometimes it's best not to complicate things, and just go with what you know.

2 oz. Jack Daniel's Old No. 7 whiskey

6 oz. ginger ale

1 lime wedge, for garnish

1 Pour the whiskey and ginger ale over ice into a glass and stir until chilled.

2 Garnish with a lime wedge (if desired) and enjoy.

Walking with Trees

Heering's nutty and slightly woody flavor plays very well on any outdoor excursion.

1 oz. Jack Daniel's Old No. 7 whiskey

¾ oz. sweet vermouth

¾ oz. Cherry Heering

1 oz. fresh orange juice

1 strip of orange peel, for garnish

1 Place the whiskey, vermouth, liqueur, and orange juice in a cocktail shaker, fill it two-thirds of the way with ice, and shake vigorously until chilled.

2 Strain over ice into a glass, garnish with a strip of orange peel (if desired), and enjoy.

Summer Citrus

If you left the bourbon at home, rum would also work well with these ingredients.

1¼ oz. bourbon

¾ oz. Honey Syrup (see page 33)

½ oz. fresh lemon juice

½ oz. grapefruit juice

Dash of Angostura Bitters

1 lemon twist, for garnish

1 Place all of the ingredients, except for the lemon twist, in a cocktail shaker, fill it two-thirds of the way with ice, and shake vigorously until chilled.

2 Strain over ice into a glass, garnish with a lemon twist (if desired), and enjoy.

The Evening Gathers

A good one to turn to once the golden hour commences and the shadows grow long.

2 oz. bourbon

¾ oz. fresh lemon juice

¾ oz. Simple Syrup (see page 11)

½ oz. dry Rosé

1 strip of lemon peel, for garnish

1 Place the bourbon, lemon juice, and syrup in a mixing glass, fill it two-thirds of the way with ice, and stir until chilled.

2 Strain over ice into a glass and top with the Rosé.

3 Garnish with a strip of lemon peel (if desired) and enjoy.

Family Meal

Don't pitch any leftover coffee from the morning. Instead, toss it in a cooler and incorporate it into this refresher.

2 oz. coffee, chilled

1½ oz. bourbon

2 oz. cola

1 orange wheel, for garnish

1 Place the coffee and bourbon in a glass, add ice, and stir gently.

2 Top with the cola, garnish with an orange wheel (if desired), and enjoy.

Hear the Wind Blow

A drink that's certain to remove the chill from your bones.

½ oz. fresh lemon juice

1 teaspoon sugar

1 bag of chai tea

6 oz. boiling water

1½ oz. bourbon

1 cinnamon stick, for garnish

1 Place the lemon juice, sugar, tea, and boiling water in a glass and let it steep for 5 minutes.

2 Remove the tea bag, discard it, and stir in the bourbon.

3 Garnish with a cinnamon stick (if desired) and enjoy.

Dirty Water

Think of this as a no-fuss Mint Julep that you can enjoy out in the middle of nowhere.

1½ oz. iced mint tea

3 sprigs of fresh mint

1 oz. bourbon

½ oz. Simple Syrup (see page 11)

1 lemon wheel, for garnish

1 Place the tea, mint, bourbon, and syrup in a cocktail shaker, fill it two-thirds of the way with ice, and shake vigorously until chilled.

2 Pour the contents of the shaker into a glass, garnish with a lemon wheel (if desired), and enjoy.

RUM

Some people dismiss rum as being too sweet, but that view is far too simplistic. In reality, rum is the most diverse spirit in the world, being produced in more than 80 countries. That dizzying number of perspectives and the long history of craftsmanship that sustain them result in a number of quality offerings that are both accessible and complex, making it a great spirit to build a campfire cocktail party around.

Hawaij Hot Cocoa

Hawaij is a Yemeni spice blend that can bring a ho-hum cup of cocoa to life.

1 cup milk

1 tablespoon sugar

½ oz. dark chocolate

1½ teaspoons (scant) cocoa powder

1 oz. rum

1 teaspoon Hawaij Spice Blend (see opposite page)

Pinch of kosher salt

1 cinnamon stick, for garnish

1 Place the milk, sugar, and chocolate in a small saucepan and warm the mixture over medium-high heat, whisking until the chocolate begins to melt.

2 Add the cocoa powder, rum, Hawaij Spice Blend, and salt and continue to whisk until the cocoa powder has been incorporated, the chocolate has melted completely, and the mixture just comes to a simmer.

3 Pour the cocoa into mugs, garnish with a cinnamon stick (if desired), and enjoy.

Hawaij Spice Blend

Place 1½ tablespoons ground ginger, 1 tablespoon cinnamon, 1½ teaspoons cardamom, ½ teaspoon ground cloves, and a pinch of freshly grated nutmeg in a mixing bowl, stir to combine, and store in an airtight container.

Dark & Stormy

The national drink of Bermuda, this is a beachy cocktail that travels well.

1½ oz. aged or black rum

⅔ oz. fresh lime juice

¼ oz. Demerara Syrup (see page 28)

2 dashes of Angostura Bitters

3 oz. ginger beer

1 lime wedge, for garnish

1 Place the rum, lime juice, syrup, and bitters in a cocktail shaker, fill it two-thirds of the way with ice, and shake vigorously until chilled.

2 Strain over ice into a glass, top with the ginger beer, garnish with a lime wedge (if desired), and enjoy.

Aire Nocturno

Simple Syrup (see page 11) can be used here, but Demerara Syrup will supply the rich mouthfeel you want.

1½ oz. rum

¾ oz. orange liqueur

1 teaspoon Luxardo maraschino liqueur

½ oz. fresh lime juice

½ teaspoon Demerara Syrup (see page 28)

1 lime wedge, for garnish

1 Place the rum, liqueurs, lime juice, and syrup in a cocktail shaker, fill it two-thirds of the way with ice, and shake vigorously until chilled.

2 Strain the cocktail into a glass, garnish with a lime wedge (if desired), and enjoy.

Walking in the Air

Straightforward with surprising depth, this cocktail will erase any of the day's discomforts.

2 oz. rum

3 oz. orange juice

½ oz. fresh lime juice

¾ oz. grenadine

1 Place the rum, orange juice, and lime juice in a cocktail shaker, fill it two-thirds of the way with ice, and shake vigorously until chilled.

2 Pour the contents of the shaker into a glass. Slowly pour the grenadine over the cocktail, and enjoy.

Analogue

There are plenty of options for falernum, but John D. Taylor's Velvet Falernum is by far the best choice.

1½ oz. rum

1 oz. bourbon

½ oz. falernum

¼ oz. ginger liqueur

¼ oz. St. Elizabeth Allspice Dram

3 dashes of Angostura Bitters

1 Place all of the ingredients in a mixing glass, fill it two-thirds of the way with ice, and stir until chilled.

2 Strain over ice into a glass and enjoy.

Thinking of You

Find yourself a quiet spot and take your time with this one, as it runs in an astonishing number of directions.

1½ oz. rum

¾ oz. pineapple juice

½ oz. fresh lemon juice

½ oz. grenadine

2 dashes of orange bitters

Dash of Angostura Bitters

1 strip of orange peel, for garnish

1 Place all of the ingredients, except for the strip of orange peel, in a cocktail shaker, fill it two-thirds of the way with ice, and shake vigorously until chilled.

2 Strain the cocktail into a glass, garnish with a strip of orange peel (if desired), and enjoy.

Mango Tango

Look for mango and pineapple juices that aren't made from concentrate—the difference in the final product will be eye-opening.

1 oz. aged rum

1 oz. coconut rum

1 oz. orange liqueur

½ oz. fresh lime juice

4 oz. mango juice

2 oz. pineapple juice

1 slice of mango, for garnish

1 Place all of the ingredients, except for the slice of mango, in a cocktail shaker, fill it two-thirds of the way with ice, and shake vigorously until chilled.

2 Pour the contents of the shaker into a glass, garnish with a slice of mango (if desired), and enjoy.

Sunburst

The grapefruit juice amplifies the tart notes in the pineapple juice, while the creamy character of the coconut rum leads to a satisfying close.

1 oz. coconut rum

1 oz. pineapple juice

2 oz. grapefruit juice

1 orange wheel, for garnish

1 Place the rum, pineapple juice, and grapefruit juice in a glass, add ice, and stir until chilled.

2 Garnish with an orange wheel (if desired) and enjoy.

Cidermeister

Though it is typically consumed as a shot, Jägermeister makes for a wonderful cocktail ingredient.

1 oz. rum

1 oz. Jägermeister

4 oz. apple cider

1 cinnamon stick, for garnish

1 Place the rum, Jägermeister, and apple cider in a glass, add ice, and stir until chilled.

2 Garnish with a cinnamon stick (if desired) and enjoy.

Bee Aggressive

The funky character of Appleton Estate Signature Blend is an excellent option for the rum here.

½ oz. honey

½ oz. pure maple syrup

1 oz. warm water

½ oz. fresh lemon juice

2 oz. aged rum

1 lemon twist, for garnish

1 Place the honey, maple syrup, and warm water in a glass and stir until the honey and syrup have dissolved.

2 Place the lemon juice and rum in a cocktail shaker, add the honey-and-syrup mixture, and fill the shaker two-thirds of the way with ice.

3 Shake vigorously until chilled and strain over ice into a glass.

4 Garnish with a lemon twist (if desired) and enjoy.

Painkiller

Overproof rum, which is also called "navy strength" from time to time, is any rum that is more than 50 percent alcohol by volume. Pusser's and Wray & Nephew are both good options.

2 oz. rum (overproof recommended)

1 oz. cream of coconut

1 oz. orange juice

4 oz. pineapple juice

Freshly grated nutmeg, for garnish

1 orange wheel, for garnish

1 Place the rum, cream of coconut, orange juice, and pineapple juice in a cocktail shaker, fill it two-thirds of the way with crushed ice, and shake until chilled.

2 Pour the contents of the shaker into a glass, garnish with nutmeg and an orange wheel (if desired), and enjoy.

Jungle Bird

A tiki classic that travels exceptionally well.

1½ oz. black rum

½ oz. Campari

1½ oz. pineapple juice

⅓ oz. fresh lime juice

2 pineapple chunks, for garnish

1 Place the rum, Campari, and juices in a cocktail shaker, fill the shaker two-thirds of the way with ice, and shake until chilled.

2 Strain over ice into a glass, garnish with pineapple chunks (if desired), and enjoy.

Day Is Done

Make two of these, sit back with a loved one, and listen to the wind in the trees.

1½ oz. white rum

1½ oz. orange liqueur

2 oz. club soda

Splash of grenadine

1 lime wedge, for garnish

1 Place the rum, liqueur, and club soda in a glass, add ice, and stir until chilled.

2 Top with the splash of grenadine, garnish with a lime wedge (if desired), and enjoy.

Rum Runner Punch

Should you have a desire to make a batch cocktail and take that along rather than a dozen different jars and bottles, this is a good choice.

1 oz. spiced rum

2 oz. orange juice

1 oz. cranberry juice

1 Place all of the ingredients in a cocktail shaker, fill it two-thirds of the way with ice, and shake vigorously until chilled.

2 Strain the cocktail over ice into a glass and enjoy.

Dance This Mess Around

Cocktail snobs would sneer at this collection of ingredients. Little do they know all the enjoyment they're missing out on.

1 oz. spiced rum

1 oz. Kahlúa

1 oz. orange liqueur

1 Place all of the ingredients in a cocktail shaker, fill it two-thirds of the way with ice, and shake vigorously until chilled.

2 Strain over ice into a glass and enjoy.

All the Hearts

A delicious and decadent cocktail that has dessert covered.

1 oz. white rum

1 oz. Kahlúa

1 oz. Irish cream liqueur

Dash of white crème de menthe

1 sprig of fresh mint, for garnish

1 Place the rum, Kahlúa, and cream liqueur in a cocktail shaker, fill it two-thirds of the way with ice, and shake vigorously until chilled.

2 Strain over ice into a glass, top with the dash of crème de menthe, garnish with a sprig of mint (if desired), and enjoy.

Slang Teacher

A trio of juices and coconut rum combine forces for a cocktail that's as fun as it is refreshing.

1½ oz. coconut rum

1½ oz. pineapple juice

¼ oz. fresh lemon juice

3 oz. grapefruit juice

1 grapefruit twist, for garnish

1 Fill a glass with ice, add the coconut rum and juices, and stir until chilled.

2 Garnish with a grapefruit twist (if desired) and enjoy.

Let's Fall in Love Tonight

Since you only need 2 drops, you might think you can forgo the Angostura here—but you would be wrong.

1 oz. dark rum

1 oz. pineapple juice

1 oz. orange juice

2 drops of Angostura Bitters

1 slice of pineapple, for garnish

1 Place the rum, juices, and bitters in a cocktail shaker, fill it two-thirds of the way with ice, and shake vigorously until chilled.

2 Strain over ice into a glass, garnish with a slice of pineapple (if desired), and enjoy.

When I Come Knocking

Rum forms the bridge between the whisky and brandy here, allowing the two bold flavors to accommodate each other.

1 oz. rum

1 oz. Crown Royal whisky

1 oz. brandy

Splash of grenadine

1 maraschino cherry, for garnish

1 Place the rum, whisky, brandy, and grenadine in a glass, add ice, and stir until chilled.

2 Garnish with a maraschino cherry (if desired) and enjoy.

Bow Tai

A pared-down take on the Mai Tai that was made for a summertime trek.

1½ oz. white rum

¾ oz. dark rum

¾ oz. orange liqueur

½ oz. fresh lime juice

1 lime wedge, for garnish

1 Place the rums, liqueur, and lime juice in a cocktail shaker, fill it two-thirds of the way with ice, and shake vigorously until chilled.

2 Strain over ice into a glass, garnish with a lime wedge (if desired), and enjoy.

TEQUILA

With their sharp bite and fruity flavors, tequila and mezcal were made for the refreshing yet inventive cocktails that a camping trip cries out for. Successfully meeting that call is dependent upon one thing: that you don't skimp. You don't need to break the bank, but opting for some bargain brand will severely limit the quality of your cocktails, so make sure that whatever spirit you purchase is 100 percent agave.

El Diablo

A drink that will make you happy to go over to the dark side.

1½ oz. tequila

1 oz. crème de cassis

½ oz. fresh lime juice

Ginger beer, to top

Fresh mint, for garnish

1 Place the tequila, liqueur, and lime juice in a cocktail shaker, fill it two-thirds of the way with ice, and shake vigorously until chilled.

2 Strain over ice into a glass and top with ginger beer.

3 Garnish with fresh mint (if desired) and enjoy.

A Cold Snap

Contrary to what you may think, tequila pairs quite well with chocolate, thanks to the natural sweetness of agave.

2 oz. tequila

2 oz. Irish cream liqueur

4 oz. hot chocolate

Marshmallows, for garnish

1 Place the tequila, liqueur, and hot chocolate in a mug and stir until well combined.

2 Garnish with marshmallows (if desired) and enjoy.

Apple Tart

Don't skimp on the schnapps; otherwise, this cocktail is in danger of becoming too sweet.

2 oz. tequila

1 oz. apple schnapps

1 oz. apple juice

½ oz. fresh lime juice

1 lime wheel, for garnish

1 Place the tequila, schnapps, apple juice, and lime juice in a mixing glass, fill it two-thirds of the way with ice, and stir until chilled.

2 Strain into a glass, garnish with a lime wheel (if desired), and enjoy.

Bloody Maria

As you might have guessed, this is just a Bloody Mary with tequila in it. But, due to that spirit's mystical energizing abilities, it's an even better bet to get you going the morning after a long night.

Tajín or chili powder, for the rim

2 oz. tequila

½ oz. olive brine

½ oz. fresh lime juice

2 dashes of horseradish

3 drops of Worcestershire sauce

3 dashes of hot sauce

2 dashes of celery salt

Tomato juice, to fill

1 If a rimmed glass is desired, wet the rim of a glass and coat it with Tajín or chili powder.

2 Fill the glass with ice, add the remaining ingredients, and stir until chilled.

3 Garnish as desired and enjoy.

Vampiro

A word to the wise: make a large batch of the Vampiro Mix before you take off—it'll save you some valuable space, and keep you from leaving any key components behind.

Tajín, for the rim

2 oz. mezcal

2 oz. Vampiro Mix (see page 108)

½ oz. fresh lime juice

2 oz. fresh grapefruit juice

¾ oz. Simple Syrup (see page 11)

Pinch of kosher salt

2 oz. seltzer

1 celery stalk, for garnish

1 If a rimmed glass is desired, wet the rim of a glass and coat it with Tajín.

2 Place the mezcal, Vampiro Mix, juices, and syrup in a cocktail shaker, add 1 ice cube, and shake vigorously until chilled.

3 Pour the cocktail into the glass and add the salt and seltzer.

4 Garnish with a celery stalk (if desired) and enjoy.

Vampiro Mix

Place 10 oz. Clamato, 1 oz. apple cider vinegar, 3 oz. fresh lime juice, 2 oz. agave nectar, 1 tablespoon sriracha, 2 teaspoons blood orange juice, 2 teaspoons smoked paprika, and 1 teaspoon black pepper in a blender, season the mixture with salt, and pulse to combine. Use immediately or store in the refrigerator.

Vampiro, see page 107

Batanga

The Mexican Coca-Cola, with its use of natural cane sugar, is the key to a properly executed version of this serve.

2 pinches of kosher salt, plus more for the rim

½ oz. fresh lime juice

2 oz. tequila

3½ oz. Mexican Coca-Cola

1 lime slice, for garnish

1 If a rimmed glass is desired, wet the rim of a glass and rim it with salt.

2 Place the lime juice and salt in the glass and stir until the salt has dissolved.

3 Add the tequila and ice, top with the soda, and gently stir to combine.

4 Garnish with a lime slice (if desired) and enjoy.

Oaxacarajillo

The ease of making coffee while camping means that you can never have enough coffee-based cocktails in your repertoire.

1½ oz. Licor 43

1 oz. mezcal

1 teaspoon agave nectar

1 oz. iced coffee

1 Place the Licor 43, mezcal, and agave nectar in a glass and add ice.

2 Slowly pour the iced coffee over the back of a spoon so that it floats atop the cocktail and enjoy.

Pillow Talk

Tequila's pleasant bite bridges the sweetness of the pineapple and the tart lemon juice and grenadine.

1¼ oz. tequila

2 oz. pineapple juice

1 oz. fresh lemon juice

¼ oz. grenadine

1 Place all of the ingredients in a cocktail shaker, fill it two-thirds of the way with ice, and shake vigorously until chilled.

2 Strain over ice into a glass and enjoy.

Mexico City

The Grand Marnier, with its bold notes of citrus and vanilla, keeps this cocktail from becoming too tart.

1¼ oz. tequila

¼ oz. Grand Marnier

½ oz. fresh lime juice

1 oz. cranberry juice

1 strip of orange peel, for garnish

1 Place the tequila, Grand Marnier, and juices in a cocktail shaker, fill it two-thirds of the way with ice, and shake vigorously until chilled.

2 Strain into a glass, garnish with a strip of orange peel (if desired), and enjoy.

Jennifer's Slipper

Dismissed as a cocktail ingredient for decades, Midori had its taste tweaked to suit the modern palate back in 2012, becoming less sweet and artificial tasting. Combine that with its enticing green hue, and it's returned to respectability over the last decade.

1 oz. tequila

½ oz. Midori

⅔ oz. fresh lemon juice

⅔ oz. fresh lime juice

1 teaspoon Simple Syrup (see page 11)

1 lemon slice, for garnish

1 Place the tequila, Midori, juices, and syrup in a cocktail shaker, fill it two-thirds of the way with ice, and shake vigorously until chilled.

2 Strain over ice into a glass, garnish with a slice of lemon (if desired), and enjoy.

Smoke on the Beach

Refreshing, but with just enough smoke to make one linger over each sip.

1 oz. mezcal

1 oz. tequila

1 oz. fresh
lime juice

1 oz. pineapple
juice

½ oz. agave nectar

1 strip of orange
peel, for garnish

1 Place the mezcal, tequila, juices, and agave nectar in a cocktail shaker, fill it two-thirds of the way with ice, and shake vigorously until chilled.

2 Strain into a glass, garnish with a strip of orange peel (if desired), and enjoy.

Margarita

The most popular cocktail in America does not lose its luster when taken out into the woods.

Salt, for the rim

2 oz. tequila

1 oz. orange liqueur

1 oz. fresh lime juice

1 lime wheel, for garnish

1 If a rimmed glass is desired, wet the rim of a glass and coat it with salt.

2 Place the tequila, orange liqueur, and lime juice in a cocktail shaker, fill it two-thirds of the way with ice, and shake vigorously until chilled.

3 Strain over ice into the glass, garnish with a lime wheel (if desired), and enjoy.

Paloma

Spanish for "dove," the Paloma provides a fitting clemency to any proceeding.

2 oz. tequila

1 oz. grapefruit juice

½ oz. fresh lime juice

Grapefruit soda, to top

1 grapefruit wedge, for garnish

1 Place the tequila, grapefruit juice, and lime juice in a glass, add ice, and stir until chilled.

2 Top with grapefruit soda and gently stir to incorporate it.

3 Garnish with a grapefruit wedge (if desired) and enjoy.

Blooming Cactus

As cool and refreshing as the evening air in Taos, New Mexico.

6 fresh mint leaves, torn, plus more for garnish

Dash of fresh lime juice

1 oz. tequila

4 oz. cranberry juice

1 Place the mint leaves and lime juice in a cocktail shaker and muddle.

2 Add ice along with the tequila and cranberry juice and shake until chilled.

3 Strain over ice into a glass filled with ice, garnish with additional mint (if desired), and enjoy.

Kinda Knew Anna

Don't mistake crème de mure as some exotic ingredient—it's simply blackberry liqueur.

1 oz. tequila

1 oz. crème de mure

1 oz. fresh lime juice

2 oz. ginger beer

1 sage leaf, for garnish

1 Place the tequila, liqueur, and lime juice in a cocktail shaker, fill it two-thirds of the way with ice, and shake vigorously until chilled.

2 Strain over ice into a glass and top with the ginger beer.

3 Garnish with a sage leaf (if desired) and enjoy.

Ranch Water

The gentle bubbles and slight salinity of Topo Chico key this simple refresher.

1 (12 oz.) bottle of Topo Chico

1½ oz. tequila

¼ oz. fresh lime juice

1 lime wedge, for garnish

1 Pour out 2 oz. of the Topo Chico and add the tequila and lime juice to the bottle.

2 Garnish with a lime wedge (if desired) and enjoy.

The Burro

Swapping tequila in for the vodka carries the Moscow Mule to unprecedented heights.

2 oz. tequila

Splash of orange liqueur

¼ oz. fresh lime juice

4 oz. ginger beer

1 lime wedge, for garnish

1 Place the tequila, liqueur, and lime juice in a glass, add ice, and stir until chilled.

2 Top with the ginger beer, garnish with a lime wedge (if desired), and enjoy.

Baja Lemonade

The rosemary ties everything together in this refreshing serve.

1 sprig of fresh rosemary

2 oz. tequila

Splash of coconut rum

4 oz. lemonade

1 lemon wheel, for garnish

1 Place the rosemary, tequila, and coconut rum in a cocktail shaker, fill it two-thirds of the way with ice, and shake vigorously until chilled.

2 Strain over ice into a glass and top with the lemonade.

3 Garnish with a lemon wheel (if desired) and enjoy.

Early Night

This reworking of the Tequila Sunrise is so delicious that you need to be careful about how quickly you take it down.

1½ oz. tequila

1½ oz. Cherry Heering

½ oz. fresh lime juice

3 oz. orange juice

1 maraschino cherry, for garnish

1 Place the tequila, liqueur, and juices in a glass, add ice, and stir until chilled.

2 Garnish with a maraschino cherry (if desired) and enjoy.

Toronha

The low acidity and powerful sweetness of the Cara Cara orange make it the best option here.

2 oz. tequila

½ oz. orange liqueur

2 oz. grapefruit juice

½ oz. fresh orange juice

Dash of grenadine

1 Place all of the ingredients in a cocktail shaker, fill it two-thirds of the way with ice, and shake vigorously until chilled.

2 Strain over ice into a glass and enjoy.

Matador

Some versions of this drink include grenadine, so don't hesitate to add about ½ oz. if the drink the components below produce isn't complex enough for you.

1¼ oz. tequila

2 oz. pineapple juice

1 oz. fresh lime juice

1 lime wheel, for garnish

1 Place the tequila and juices in a cocktail shaker, fill it two-thirds of the way with ice, and shake until chilled.

2 Strain into a glass, garnish with a lime wheel (if desired), and enjoy.

Set It Off

The nutty, slightly smoky flavor of Luxardo makes it a lovely partner for mezcal.

½ oz. Hibiscus Syrup (see opposite page)

¾ oz. fresh lemon juice

¼ oz. Luxardo maraschino liqueur

1½ oz. mezcal

1 Place the syrup, lemon juice, liqueur, and mezcal in a cocktail shaker, fill it two-thirds of the way with ice, and shake vigorously until chilled.

2 Strain into a glass and enjoy.

Hibiscus Syrup

Place ¼ cup dried hibiscus blossoms and 2 cups Demerara Syrup (see page 28) in a large mason jar and let the mixture steep at room temperature for 6 hours. Strain the syrup and use immediately or store in the refrigerator.

GIN

After a long day of hiking, gathering wood, and prepping the evening meal, a refreshing cocktail is called for. And when refreshing is the focus, gin is the go-to. Its light and aromatic nature lends itself to drinks that are both breezy and intriguing, plus its slightly piney flavor makes it a natural for outdoor imbibing.

Gin & Tonic

Bring along a quality tonic, such as Fever-Tree, when you're in the mood for this summer standby.

2½ oz. gin

2½ oz. tonic water

Splash of fresh lime juice

1 lime wedge, for garnish

1 Fill a glass with ice, add the gin and tonic water, and stir until chilled.

2 Top with the lime juice, garnish with a lime wedge (if desired), and enjoy.

Bee's Knees

If you're looking for a little more out of this one, try swapping in fresh orange juice for some portion of the lemon juice.

---

2 oz. gin

¾ oz. fresh lemon juice

¾ oz. Honey Syrup (see page 33)

1 lemon twist, for garnish

1 Place the gin, lemon juice, and syrup in a cocktail shaker, fill it two-thirds of the way with ice, and shake vigorously until chilled.

2 Strain into a glass, garnish with a lemon twist (if desired), and enjoy.

Gin Basil Smash

Originally named the Gin Pesto, this refreshing, aromatic wonder swept around the globe shortly after Jörg Meyer created it at Paris' Le Lion in 2008.

12 fresh basil leaves

2 oz. gin

¾ oz. fresh lime juice

⅓ oz. Simple Syrup (see page 11)

1 sprig of fresh basil, for garnish

1 Place the basil leaves in a cocktail shaker and muddle them. Add the gin, lime juice, and syrup, fill the shaker two-thirds of the way with ice, and shake vigorously until chilled.

2 Strain over ice into a glass, garnish with a sprig of basil (if desired), and enjoy.

The Elder Fashion

St-Germain is also known as "bartender's ketchup," due to its ability to improve every cocktail it touches.

2 oz. gin

½ oz. St-Germain

Dash of orange bitters

1 lime wheel, for garnish

1 Place the gin, St-Germain, and bitters in a mixing glass, fill it two-thirds of the way with ice, and stir until chilled.

2 Strain over ice into a glass, garnish with a lime wheel (if desired), and enjoy.

Arch Leaves

Any time a cocktail can unite strong flavors like gin, orange juice, and sambuca, you can be confident a good time awaits.

1 oz. gin

1 oz. fresh orange juice

½ oz. sambuca

½ oz. dry vermouth

1 Place all of the ingredients in a cocktail shaker, fill it two-thirds of the way with ice, and shake vigorously until chilled.

2 Strain into a glass and enjoy.

Docile Cobra

The fiery flavor of Barrow's sparks this riff on the Bee's Knees.

¾ oz. gin

¾ oz. Barrow's Intense Ginger Liqueur

¾ oz. fresh lemon juice

¼ oz. Honey Syrup (see page 33)

1 lemon wedge, for garnish

1 Place the gin, liqueur, lemon juice, and syrup in a cocktail shaker, fill it two-thirds of the way with ice, and shake vigorously until chilled.

2 Pour the contents of the shaker into a glass, garnish with a lemon wedge (if desired), and enjoy.

Gin Blossom

A fun spin on the Tom Collins, cutting back on the sweetness to let the tart elements shine.

1½ oz. gin

1½ oz. orange liqueur

3 oz. club soda

Splash of grenadine

1 orange twist, for garnish

1 Add the gin and liqueur to a glass filled with ice.

2 Add the club soda and stir until chilled.

3 Add the grenadine and let it slowly filter down into the cocktail.

4 Garnish with an orange twist (if desired) and enjoy.

Gin & Juice

See why Snoop Dogg made such a fuss about this amalgam in one of his many mid-'90s anthems.

2 oz. gin

2 oz. cranberry juice

Splash of orange liqueur

½ oz. fresh lime juice

1 lime wheel, for garnish

1 Place the gin, cranberry juice, liqueur, and lime juice in a cocktail shaker, fill it two-thirds of the way with ice, and shake vigorously until chilled.

2 Strain over ice into a glass, garnish with a lime wheel (if desired), and enjoy.

Greyhound

As the name suggests, this one is speedy to make, and sleek on the palate.

2 oz. gin

4 oz. grapefruit juice

1 grapefruit twist, for garnish

1 Fill a glass with ice, add the gin and grapefruit juice, and stir until chilled.

2 Garnish with a grapefruit twist (if desired) and enjoy.

South Side

It is rumored that this cocktail is tied to Al Capone's gang on the South Side of Chicago, where folks were desperate to smooth out the coarse gin Capone and his men were bringing in.

2 oz. gin

Splash of limoncello

⅔ oz. Simple Syrup (see page 11)

½ oz. fresh lemon juice

4 fresh mint leaves

1 lemon slice, for garnish

1 Place the gin, limoncello, syrup, lemon juice, and mint in a cocktail shaker, fill it two-thirds of the way with ice, and shake vigorously until chilled.

2 Strain over ice into a glass, garnish with a lemon slice (if desired), and enjoy.

Negroni

As Kingsley Amis, the great English author and spirits aficionado, once said of the Negroni, "It has the power, rare with drinks and indeed with anything else, of cheering you up."

⅔ oz. Campari

⅔ oz. sweet vermouth

2 oz. gin

1 orange slice, for garnish

1 Place the Campari, sweet vermouth, and gin in a mixing glass, fill the glass two-thirds of the way with ice, and stir until chilled.

2 Strain over ice into a glass, garnish with an orange slice (if desired), and enjoy.

The Church

The crisp flavor of Cocchi Americano makes this a cocktail worthy of worshipping.

1 oz. Aperol

1 oz. gin

1 oz. fresh lemon juice

½ oz. Demerara Syrup (see page 28)

½ oz. Cocchi Americano

1 orange wheel, for garnish

1 Place the Aperol, gin, lemon juice, syrup, and Cocchi Americano in a cocktail shaker, fill it two-thirds of the way with ice, and shake vigorously until chilled.

2 Strain over ice into a glass, garnish with an orange wheel (if desired), and enjoy.

Watermelon Stand

Aperol is smoother than most bitter apertifs, with woody notes that make it a good fit for sitting and soaking up the beautiful scent of woodsmoke in the outdoors.

4 watermelon chunks

1½ oz. gin

¾ oz. fresh lemon juice

½ oz. Simple Syrup (see page 11)

½ oz. Aperol

1 Place the watermelon and gin in a cocktail shaker and muddle.

2 Add the remaining ingredients and ice and shake vigorously until chilled.

3 Strain over ice into a glass and enjoy.

Big Bend Fizz

A gorgeous cocktail that brings to mind the sunset in the remote Texas wilderness that lends its name to the drink.

1½ oz. gin

½ oz. fresh lemon juice

¾ oz. fresh orange juice

¼ oz. grenadine

2 oz. Champagne, chilled

1 orange twist, for garnish

1 Place the gin, juices, and grenadine in a cocktail shaker, fill it two-thirds of the way with ice, and shake vigorously until chilled.

2 Strain into a glass and top with the Champagne.

3 Garnish with an orange twist (if desired) and enjoy.

VODKA

Vodka can get a bad rap due to its neutral flavor, but that quality is a major plus when the time comes to make cocktails in the great outdoors. Simply put, vodka doesn't need too much else alongside it to make an enjoyable cocktail. As a large part of camping is cutting away complication, these cocktails are a great fit for the great outdoors.

Hairy Navel

The name may conjure memories of the bygone '70s, but the flavor is eternally enjoyable.

1½ oz. vodka

1½ oz. peach schnapps

4 oz. orange juice

Splash of pineapple juice

1 orange slice, for garnish

1 Place the vodka, schnapps, and juices in a cocktail shaker, fill it two-thirds of the way with ice, and shake vigorously until chilled.

2 Strain over ice into a glass, garnish with an orange slice (if desired), and enjoy.

Screwdriver

With only two ingredients required and the potential to work any time of day, the Screwdriver is a strong contender to become the go-to cocktail of the outdoor enthusiast.

2 oz. vodka

4 oz. orange juice

1 orange slice, for garnish

1 Fill a glass with ice, add the vodka and orange juice, and stir until chilled.

2 Garnish with an orange slice (if desired) and enjoy.

Screwdriver, see page 167

Citrus Sunset

If you have an option, opt for ruby red grapefruit juice here.

1 oz. vodka

4 oz. grapefruit juice

½ oz. fresh lime juice

¼ oz. fresh lemon juice

Splash of grenadine

1 lime slice, for garnish

1 Place the vodka, juices, and grenadine in a cocktail shaker, fill it two-thirds of the way with ice, and shake vigorously until chilled.

2 Strain over ice into a glass, garnish with a slice of lime (if desired), and enjoy.

Moscow Mule

Don't fret about packing copper mugs. There will be those who insist that one is necessary for a Moscow Mule. But don't hesitate to respond, "Camping is all about adapting."

4 fresh mint leaves

½ oz. fresh
lime juice

2 oz. vodka

6 oz. ginger beer

1 lime wedge,
for garnish

1 Place the mint leaves and lime juice in a glass and add ice.

2 Add the vodka and top with the ginger beer.

3 Garnish with a lime wedge (if desired) and enjoy.

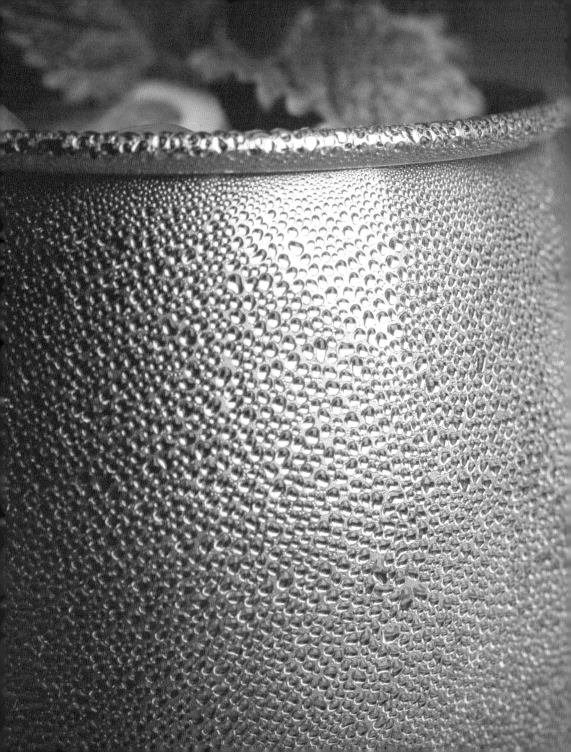

Moscow Mule, see page 171

Bloody Mary

No need to restrict this to the morning hours: the Bloody Mary proves restorative and refreshing all day.

½ oz. fresh
lime juice

2 oz. vodka

½ oz. olive brine

2 dashes of
horseradish

3 drops of
Worcestershire
sauce

3 dashes of
hot sauce

Dash of
black pepper

2 dashes of
celery salt

Tomato juice, to top

1 Place all of the ingredients, except for the tomato juice, in a glass, add ice, and stir until chilled.

2 Top with tomato juice and gently stir.

3 Garnish as desired and enjoy.

Heliopause

A cocktail for those evenings where you first start to feel summer giving way to fall.

6 oz. orange juice

1 oz. vodka

1 oz. orange liqueur

1 oz. crème de cassis

1 orange wheel, for garnish

1 Place the orange juice, vodka, and orange liqueur in a cocktail shaker, fill it two-thirds of the way with ice, and shake vigorously until chilled.

2 Strain over ice into a glass, add the crème de cassis, and let it filter down into the drink.

3 Garnish with an orange wheel (if desired) and enjoy.

Old Fashioned Apple Pie

This drink can be served hot or cold. If you need something warm, simply place the ingredients in a pan and bring them to a simmer over the fire. Pour the mix into your mug and enjoy.

1½ oz. vanilla vodka

Dash of Demerara Syrup (see page 28)

3 oz. apple cider

3 oz. apple juice

Cinnamon, for garnish

1 Place the vodka, syrup, apple cider, and apple juice in a cocktail shaker, fill it two-thirds of the way with ice, and shake vigorously until chilled.

2 Strain over ice into a glass, garnish with a dusting of cinnamon (if desired), and enjoy.

Arctic Warmer

If you don't like the idea of butter in a beverage, you can substitute cream or milk. Just be aware that this will change the flavor of the drink quite a bit, and not necessarily for the better.

4 oz. hot tea

1 teaspoon unsalted butter

1½ oz. vodka

½ oz. tequila

Dash of cinnamon

1 cinnamon stick, for garnish

1 Place the tea, butter, vodka, tequila, and cinnamon in a glass and stir until combined.

2 Garnish with a cinnamon stick (if desired) and enjoy.

White Russian

Milk and half-and-half can both work here, but heavy cream tastes best, and you can afford the extra calories after the day's hike.

2 oz. vodka

1 oz. Kahlúa

Heavy cream, to taste

1 Place a few ice cubes in a glass, add the vodka and Kahlúa, and stir until chilled.

2 Top with a generous splash of heavy cream, slowly stir until combined, and enjoy.

Harvey Wallbanger

Fresh orange juice is the key to restoring this cocktail to the glory of its heyday, which came during the 1970s.

3 oz. fresh orange juice

1¼ oz. vodka

½ oz. Galliano

1 orange slice, for garnish

1 Place the orange juice and vodka in a glass, add ice, and stir until chilled.

2 Float the Galliano on top by slowly pouring it over the back of a spoon, garnish with an orange slice (if desired), and enjoy.

Blue Lagoon

Yes, it's as refreshing as it looks in the glass.

1½ oz. vodka

1½ oz. blue
Curaçao

6 oz. lemonade

Dash of fresh
lime juice

1 lemon slice,
for garnish

1 Place the vodka and blue Curaçao in a cocktail
shaker, fill it two-thirds of the way with ice, and shake
vigorously until chilled.

2 Strain over ice into a glass, top with the lemonade and
lime juice, and gently stir to combine.

3 Garnish with a slice of lemon (if desired) and enjoy.

Feel Flows

The subtle spice and sweetness from the ginger ale tie everything together here.

2 oz. vodka

Splash of orange liqueur

2 oz. grapefruit juice

4 oz. ginger ale

1 lime wheel, for garnish

1 Fill a glass with ice, add the vodka, liqueur, and grapefruit juice, and stir until chilled.

2 Top with the ginger ale and gently stir to combine.

3 Garnish with a lime wheel (if desired) and enjoy.

Great Idea

A drink that came together after experimenting with what little liquor was on hand, and ended up being a brilliant move.

1½ oz. vodka

1½ oz. Jägermeister

¾ oz. fresh lemon juice

1 lemon wheel, for garnish

1 Place the vodka, Jägermeister, and lemon juice in a glass and gently stir to combine.

2 Add ice to the glass and stir until chilled.

3 Garnish with a lemon wheel (if desired) and enjoy.

You Know, You Know

If you want to play up the saline notes of Topo Chico even more, rim the glasses with salt.

1½ oz. vodka

2 oz. fresh lemon juice

Topo Chico, to top

1 lemon wheel, for garnish

1 Add ice to a glass along with the vodka and lemon juice. Top with Topo Chico and stir until chilled.

2 Garnish with a lemon wheel (if desired) and enjoy.

Seabreeze

Some recipes for the Seabreeze will include 1 oz. fresh lime juice, so give that a try if you're looking for a little something more from this drink. Shaking the ingredients instead of simply building the cocktail in the glass has also found favor with certain folks.

2 oz. vodka

4 oz. cranberry juice

2 oz. grapefruit juice

1 grapefruit slice, for garnish

1 Place the vodka, cranberry juice, and grapefruit juice in a glass, add ice, and stir until chilled.

2 Garnish with a slice of grapefruit (if desired) and enjoy.

Borrowed Thyme

The duo of thyme and grapefruit sings a surprisingly sweet song.

2 oz. vodka

6 oz. grapefruit juice

2 oz. club soda

3 sprigs of fresh thyme

1 Place all of the ingredients in a glass, fill it with ice, stir until chilled, and enjoy.

Jungle Punch

A straightforward serve that will provide refreshment and enjoyment all weekend long.

1½ oz. vodka

1½ oz. Sprite

3 oz. fruit punch

Fresh mint, for garnish

1 Place all of the ingredients in a glass and add ice.

2 Stir until chilled, garnish with mint (if desired), and enjoy.

Amelia

A streamlined take on the Bramble, cutting back on the complication while still providing the same fruity and fresh flavor.

1½ oz. vodka

5 blackberries

¾ oz. St-Germain

½ oz. fresh lemon juice

Fresh mint, for garnish

1 Place the vodka and blackberries in a cocktail shaker and muddle.

2 Add the St-Germain and lemon juice, fill the shaker two-thirds of the way with ice, and shake vigorously until chilled.

3 Strain over ice into a glass, garnish with mint (if desired), and enjoy.

Pray Up, Stay Up

Its ability to allow Heering, Cointreau, and aromatic bitters to work together exhibits why vodka is an underrated cocktail ingredient.

1¾ oz. vodka

½ oz. Cherry Heering

4 drops of Cointreau

3 drops of Angostura Bitters

1 Place all of the ingredients in a mixing glass, fill it two-thirds of the way with ice, and stir until chilled.

2 Strain into a glass and enjoy.

WINE & OTHER SPIRITS

The spirits the previous chapters are centered around will always get most of the attention when cocktail hour arrives, but liqueur, wine, and beer should not be overlooked. From sprucing up that beer with some whiskey and lemonade to make a shandy to a fruit and flavor–packed sangria that can please a big crowd, the cocktails collected in this chapter will help you keep things fresh on your next excursion.

Garibaldi

Bitter Campari entwines itself beautifully around an orange's sweetness.

1½ oz. Campari

Fresh orange juice, to top

1 orange wedge, for garnish

1 Place 2 ice cubes in a glass, add the Campari and a splash of orange juice, and stir to combine.

2 Add 1 more ice cube and fill the glass with more orange juice.

3 Garnish with an orange wedge (if desired) and enjoy.

Campfire S'mores

If you happen to be able to find one locally, a marshmallow-flavored milk stout will be dynamite here.

Graham cracker crumbs, for the rim

Chocolate shavings, for the rim

1½ oz. bourbon

1½ oz. white crème de cacao

12 oz. stout, to top

1 toasted marshmallow, for garnish

1 If a rimmed glass is desired, place the graham cracker crumbs and chocolate shavings in a dish and stir to combine. Wet the rim of a glass and dip it into the mixture.

2 Place the bourbon and crème de cacao in a cocktail shaker, fill it two-thirds of the way with ice, and shake vigorously until chilled.

3 Strain into the glass and top with the stout.

4 Garnish with a toasted marshmallow (if desired) and enjoy.

Ausencia

Cynar, an amaro centered around the artichoke, beautifully balances its bitterness with notes of caramel, toffee, and cinnamon.

2 oz. Cynar

4 oz. grapefruit juice

4 fresh mint leaves, torn

Topo Chico, to top

1 sprig of fresh mint, for garnish

1 Place the Cynar, grapefruit juice, and mint leaves in a mixing glass, fill it two-thirds of the way with ice, and stir until chilled.

2 Strain over ice into a glass and top with Topo Chico.

3 Garnish with a sprig of mint (if desired) and enjoy.

Green Goddess Punch

"The green fairy" has lost some of her sinister reputation, opening the door to delicious drinks such as this.

1 oz. absinthe

1 oz. fresh
lime juice

1 oz. Simple Syrup
(see page 11)

4 oz. Topo Chico

1 lemon twist,
for garnish

1 Place the absinthe, lime juice, and syrup in a glass, add ice, and stir until chilled.

2 Top with the Topo Chico, garnish with a lemon twist (if desired), and enjoy.

Mimosa

The rare cocktail that is as comfortable carrying an elegant brunch as it is in the middle of the woods.

3 oz. orange juice

3 oz. Champagne

1 Place the orange juice in a glass and top with the Champagne.

2 Gently stir and enjoy.

Israeli Iced Tea

A spin on the Long Island Iced Tea, with arak changing the boozy original into a flavorful and herbaceous drink.

1½ oz. arak

¼ oz. gin

¼ oz. tequila

¼ oz. vodka

¼ oz. triple sec

1 oz. fresh lemon juice

Coca-Cola, to top

1 lemon wedge, for garnish

1 Place the spirits and lemon juice in a glass, add ice, and top with Coca-Cola.

2 Gently stir until chilled, garnish with a lemon wedge (if desired), and enjoy.

Red Buck's Fizz

The light-bodied character and fresh flavor of Prosecco allows the floral and tart elements of blood orange juice to shine in this twist on the Mimosa.

2 oz. Prosecco

1 oz. blood orange juice

1 Place the Prosecco in a glass, top with the blood orange juice, and enjoy.

Apple Toddy

Enjoy this one in the interlude between the end of the day's activities and the evening meal, as calvados is famous for invigorating the palate.

2 oz. calvados

1 teaspoon maple syrup

3 oz. hot cinnamon-apple tea

1 lemon wheel, for garnish

1 star anise, for garnish

1 Place the calvados, maple syrup, and tea in a mug and stir to combine.

2 Garnish with a lemon wheel and a star anise (if desired) and enjoy.

Tom Thumb's Blues

Old Tom is a sweeter, less aromatic variety of gin that all but disappeared during the twentieth century, but has enjoyed a recent resurgence due to its agreeable nature when used in cocktails.

2 oz. sweet vermouth

1 oz. Old Tom gin

½ teaspoon Luxardo maraschino liqueur

2 dashes of Angostura Bitters

1 lemon twist, for garnish

1 Place the vermouth, gin, liqueur, and bitters in a mixing glass, fill it two-thirds of the way with ice, and stir until chilled.

2 Strain into a glass, garnish with a lemon twist (if desired), and enjoy.

Summer Shandy

The ideal way to amplify the crisp and refreshing nature of an ice-cold beer.

8 oz. beer

4 oz. lemonade

1 lemon wedge, for garnish

1 Pour the beer into a glass and top with the lemonade.

2 Garnish with a lemon wedge (if desired) and enjoy.

Summer Shandy, see page 217

Lemon Cooler

For those moments when you want a beer, but also want a little more complexity and kick.

8 oz. Summer Shandy (see page 217)

1 oz. whiskey

1 teaspoon honey

Splash of fresh lemon juice

1 lemon slice, for garnish

1 Place the shandy in a glass and add ice.

2 Add the whiskey, honey, and lemon juice and stir to combine.

3 Garnish with a slice of lemon (if desired) and enjoy.

Michelada

A drink so good that it just may supplant the Bloody Mary as the go-to morning serve.

Salt or Tajín,
for the rim

4 oz. tomato juice

Splash of fresh
lime juice

Splash of
Worcestershire
sauce

Splash of hot sauce

4 oz. Mexican lager

1 lime wedge,
for garnish

1 If a rimmed glass is desired, wet the rim of a glass and coat it with salt or Tajín.

2 Place the tomato juice, lime juice, Worcestershire sauce, and hot sauce in the glass, add ice, and stir to combine.

3 Top with the lager, garnish with a lime wedge (if desired), and enjoy.

Americano

This one inclines toward the chillier seasons, but a dash of Suze is all it takes to make it work in the summer.

1 oz. Campari

1 oz. sweet vermouth

1 oz. orange liqueur

6 oz. club soda

1 orange slice, for garnish

1 Place the Campari, sweet vermouth, and orange liqueur in a glass, add ice, and stir until chilled.

2 Top with the club soda and gently stir.

3 Garnish with an orange slice (if desired) and enjoy.

Alabama Slammer

As potent and entertaining as the Tide under Nick Saban.

¾ oz. peach
schnapps

¾ oz. Amaretto

¾ oz. sloe gin

¾ oz. vodka

6 oz. orange juice

Splash of grenadine

1 orange slice,
for garnish

1 Place the schnapps, Amaretto, gin, and vodka in a
glass, add ice, and stir to combine.

2 Add the orange juice and grenadine and stir
until chilled.

3 Garnish with an orange slice (if desired) and enjoy.

Classic Red Sangria

When selecting wine for sangria, go with something mid-shelf. You don't want to waste a good bottle, but you also don't want to be left trying to cover the many flaws of some rotgut.

2 (750 ml) bottles of red wine

1½ cups brandy

1 cup Simple Syrup (see page 11)

1 cup orange juice

2 apples, cored, seeded, and diced

2 oranges, peeled and sliced thin

5 lemon wheels

5 lime wheels

1 Place all of the ingredients in a large, airtight container and seal.

2 Chill for 24 hours to allow the flavors to combine and pour the sangria into glasses when ready to serve.

Cozy Christmas

A good one for those outdoor enthusiasts who understand that winter is the best time of them all.

2 (750 ml) bottles of dry red wine

4 apples, cores removed, deseeded, and diced

2 oranges, sliced thin

½ cup apple vodka

2 cups apple cider

Dash of cinnamon

Pomegranate seeds, for garnish

1 Place all of the ingredients, except for the pomegranate seeds, in a large, airtight container. Chill for 4 or more hours.

2 Serve over ice, garnish with pomegranate seeds (if desired), and enjoy.

In a Pear Tree

If you prefer a slightly less sweet sangria, swap out half of the cream soda for root beer.

2 (750 ml) bottles of dry red wine

4 pears, cores removed, deseeded, and diced

3 cups seedless grapes, frozen

3 cups orange juice

1 (12 oz.) can of cream soda

1 Place all of the ingredients, except for the soda, in a large, airtight container. Chill for 4 or more hours.

2 Add the soda and gently stir.

3 Serve over ice and enjoy.

Dance of Twinkle & Shadow

Pinot Noir, with its characteristic notes of dark fruit, is by far the best red to utilize here.

2 (750 ml) bottles of dry red wine

2 plums, pits removed, sliced thin

1 cup cherries, pits removed, halved

1 cup blackberries

½ cup Grand Marnier

4 cups seltzer

1 Place all of the ingredients, except for the seltzer, in a large, airtight container. Chill for 4 or more hours.

2 When ready to serve, add the seltzer and gently stir.

3 Serve over ice and enjoy.

Firewalker

The Ginger Syrup supplies a subtle kick that works surprisingly well in sangria.

2 (750 ml) bottles of dry white wine

2 cups seedless red grapes, halved

4 plums, pits removed, diced

¾ cup Ginger Syrup (see below)

2 cups seltzer

1 Place all of the ingredients, except for the seltzer, in a large, airtight container. Chill for 4 or more hours.

2 Add the seltzer and gently stir.

3 Serve over ice and enjoy.

Ginger Syrup

Place 1 cup sugar and 1 cup water in a saucepan and bring them to a boil, stirring to dissolve the sugar. Remove the pan from heat, stir in ¼ cup peeled and thinly sliced fresh ginger, and let the mixture steep for 2 hours. Strain before using or storing in the refrigerator.

Who Knows Where the Time Goes

Tanqueray and Bombay are two solid choices for the gin here, as their flavors go wonderfully with berries.

1 cup fresh lemon juice

½ cup gin

24 blackberries

12 raspberries

2 (750 ml) bottles of sparkling wine, chilled

1 Place the lemon juice and gin in a pitcher and stir to combine.

2 Divide this mixture and the berries among glasses, top with the sparkling wine, and enjoy.

METRIC CONVERSIONS

US Measurement	Approximate Metric Liquid Measurement	Approximate Metric Dry Measurement
1 teaspoon	5 ml	5 g
1 tablespoon or ½ ounce	15 ml	14 g
1 ounce or ⅛ cup	30 ml	29 g
¼ cup or 2 ounces	60 ml	57 g
⅓ cup	80 ml	76 g
½ cup or 4 ounces	120 ml	113 g
⅔ cup	160 ml	151 g
¾ cup or 6 ounces	180 ml	170 g
1 cup or 8 ounces or ½ pint	240 ml	227 g
1½ cups or 12 ounces	350 ml	340 g
2 cups or 1 pint or 16 ounces	475 ml	454 g
3 cups or 1½ pints	700 ml	680 g
4 cups or 2 pints or 1 quart	950 ml	908 g

INDEX

ABOUT CIDER MILL PRESS
BOOK PUBLISHERS

✳ ✳ ✳

Good ideas ripen with time. From seed to harvest,
Cider Mill Press brings fine reading, information,
and entertainment together between the covers of its
creatively crafted books. Our Cider Mill bears fruit twice
a year, publishing a new crop of titles each spring and fall.

"Where Good Books Are Ready for Press"

501 Nelson Place
Nashville, Tennessee 37214
cidermillpress.com